ARLINGTON

∿ THE STORY OF OUR NATION'S CEMETERY ∿

Written and Illustrated by

CHRIS
DEMAREST

ROARING BROOK PRESS ∿ NEW YORK

For my father

Published by Flash Point, an imprint of Roaring Brook Press
Roaring Brook Press is a division of Holtzbrinck Publishing Holdings Limited Partnership
175 Fifth Avenue, New York, New York 10010
mackids.com

Cataloging-in-Publication Data is on file at the Library of Congress

Roaring Brook Press books are available for special promotions and premiums.
For details contact: Director of Special Markets, Holtzbrinck Publishers.

Photograph on page 31: Picture History. Used by permission.

First Edition November 2010

Printed in China by RR Donnelley Asia Printing Solutions Ltd., Dongguan City, Guangdong Province

10 9 8 7 6 5 4 3

ACROSS THE POTOMAC RIVER FROM WASHINGTON, D.C.,
stands Arlington National Cemetery, the final resting place of tens of thousands of Americans who have served their country. On 264 acres of rolling, wooded landscape rising above the river lie soldiers, sailors, marines, and airmen, many of whom gave their lives in defense of our nation—together with other prominent Americans who served, from presidents and Supreme Court justices to scientists, explorers, and sportsmen.

Today a carefully tended oasis of reverence and calm, Arlington has a complicated, sometimes troubled history. This is its story.

George Washington Parke Custis was less than a year old in 1781 when his father died of camp fever while serving as an aide to General George Washington. With his mother left alone to raise four children, the infant boy and his next oldest sibling, Eleanor, were adopted by their grandmother, Martha Washington and step-grandfather George Washington. For the next twenty years, Parke Custis grew up on the Washingtons' Mt. Vernon estate under the doting tutelage of the nation's first president.

After the deaths of George Washington, in 1799, and Martha three years later, George Washington Parke Custis, now twenty-one years old, began a new chapter in his life. In 1802, on land inherited from his late father, he began building what he would eventually call Arlington House. Set on a hilltop overlooking the Potomac River facing the nation's capital, this structure was to be both his home and a personal shrine to his late step-grandfather. Parke Custis would fill the house with his own paintings depicting Washington's life and deeds and with other memorabilia of his hero.

Two years into the construction of Arlington House, which took until 1818 to complete, George Washington Parke Custis married Mary Lee "Molly" Fitzhugh. In 1808 a daughter, Mary Anna Randolph, was born. Of the three children from the marriage, she was the only one to survive past the age of three.

As Mary grew into adulthood, prospective suitors began visiting Arlington House hoping for her hand in marriage. One was a controversial but colorful fellow Virginian, Sam Houston, who would rise through military life and later serve as governor of Texas. Another, also a Virginian and a childhood playmate of Mary's, was a West Point (United States Military Academy) graduate. In 1831 at the age of twenty-three, Mary Anna married the dashing army officer. His name was Robert E. Lee.

Mary Anna and Robert E. Lee moved into Arlington House after their marriage and would live there for the next thirty years. When George Washington Parke Custis died, in 1857, he left the property, now known as the Custis-Lee Mansion, to Mary and her children.

In the fall of 1859 Lee, now a general, was ordered to lead a detachment of marines and militia to Harpers Ferry, Virginia, where a radical abolitionist named John Brown was holding hostages in an attempt to start a rebellion that would end slavery. Lee and his men descended on the small river coast town and arrested Brown, who was later hung for his actions.

Tension between the northern and southern states was mounting. On April 12, 1861, breakaway southern, or Confederate, forces began a cannon bombardment of Federal troops garrisoned at Fort Sumpter in Charleston Harbor. When the news reached President Lincoln, he offered Lee the command of the Federal troops with orders to put down the uprising. Well into the night of April 19, 1861, Lee struggled with his decision. He was a loyal army officer—but also a loyal Virginian, and with the outbreak of the Civil War Virginia had seceded from the Union and joined the Confederacy. In the early hours of the following morning, Lee descended the stairs of Arlington House with a letter to Lincoln declaring his resignation from the U.S. Army. Within days he was bound for Richmond and eventual command of the Confederate Army. Mary and the couple's children followed when word of a Union attack on her home reached her. Federal troops soon crossed the Potomac River and occupied Arlington and the surrounding area. Neither she nor Lee would ever set foot in Arlington House again.

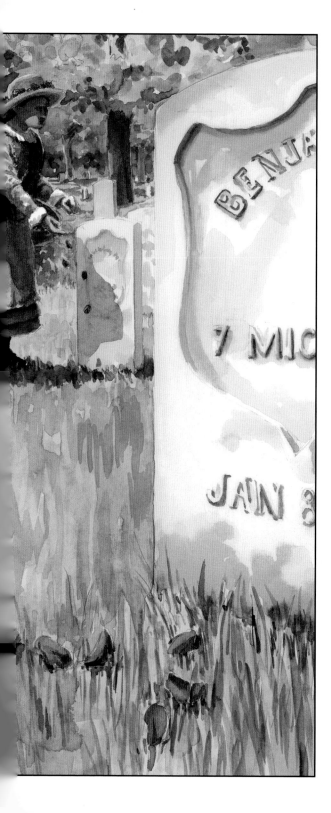

Arlington House became a symbol of resentment among the Union Army over Lee's desertion. As the Civil War progressed and Union casualties mounted, the government was running out of space in the Capital area in which to bury its war dead. As Quartermaster of the Army, Brigadier General Montgomery Meigs was in charge of supplies for the war effort—including burial space. In the summer of 1864, he proposed that Arlington be turned into a military cemetery. A southerner himself but loyal to the Union, Miegs ordered the first northern troops buried around the mansion as a punishment for what he considered Lee's treason. Among the first to be buried there was Miegs's own son, killed in action that same year.

By the end of the Civil War in 1865, 15,000 soldiers had been buried at Arlington. Three years later, in 1868, President Andrew Johnson declared May 30 Decoration Day (later to become Memorial Day), a federal holiday to honor those who had given their lives to what they believed to be a just cause. At cemeteries all across the nation, respect was paid to fallen soldiers. At Arlington, children from the Soldiers' and Sailors' Orphanage wore black sashes and walked the grounds near and around Arlington House, scattering flower petals on the graves.

Born during the Civil War, Arlington would become the last resting place for soldiers from all America's conflicts, including the Revolutionary War. In 1892 three veterans of the Revolutionary War were reburied at Arlington. Several more would follow over subsequent years.

In January of 1898 the battleship U.S.S. *Maine* was sent to Havana, Cuba, to protect American interests in Cuba's revolt against Spain. On February 15, the ship's forward powder magazines exploded, killing more than 260 sailors and marines—more than two-thirds of the crew. The exact cause of the explosion was never determined but two months later the U.S. declared war on Spain, beginning the Spanish-American War.

On December 28, 1899, the flag-draped coffins of 163 victims of the *Maine* explosion were simultaneously lowered into the ground in a special section at Arlington. Several years later, the mast was salvaged from the sunken wreck and in 1913, dedication of a new monument took place, the ship's icon now rising above its fallen crew.

Between 1917 and 1918, World War I claimed more than 100,000 American soldiers' lives. As in other wars, many of the dead were never identified. To acknowledge these "unknowns," a monument was built at Arlington into which an unidentified soldier's body would be placed. In March 1921, on his last day in office, President Woodrow Wilson signed a resolution establishing the Tomb of the Unknowns. On Memorial Day at a quiet ceremony in France, a highly decorated U.S. army sergeant by the name of Edward Younger was presented with four caskets containing the remains of unidentified World War I soldiers and asked to choose one. "Something pulled me," he recalled as he stepped forward and placed a single white rose on one casket. "This is a pal of yours," he heard.

On November 11, Veterans Day, that same year, President Warren G. Harding presided over a ceremony in the plaza of the newly completed Arlington Memorial Amphitheater dedicating the Tomb of the Unknowns. For ten years, the unknown soldier lay beneath a simple smooth white marble slab. Later, a large sarcophagus was added bearing the inscription: "Here rests in honored glory an American Soldier known but to God."

The guarding of the Tomb of the Unknowns began in 1921 by civilian watchmen and was taken over by the military five years later. At first, the guard was posted only during visiting hours at the cemetery, but in 1937 soldiers began guarding the unknowns in all weather, day and night, twenty-four hours, seven days a week. In 1948, the 3rd Army Infantry of Fort Myer, known as "The Old Guard," was given permanent watch at the tomb.

In 1956, President Dwight D. Eisenhower signed a bill to include the burial of unknown soldiers from World War II and Korea. Interred in front of the larger monument in the Amphitheater plaza, the two unknowns were each presented the Medal of Honor and laid to rest beneath marble tablets. On Memorial Day, 1984, they were joined by a fourth unknown from the Vietnam War. But with advances in DNA testing, the fourth unknown was later identified. His remains were exhumed and reinterred in his home state, and that crypt now remains empty with the inscription: "Honoring and keeping faith with America's servicemen 1958–1975."

The death of an officer in battle was once signaled by reversing his boots in his stirrups and sending his horse back to head-quarters. This old military custom continues to this day in the tradition of the riderless or caparisoned horse at the funerals of high-ranking officers and heads of state. The first noteworthy use of the caparisoned horse in the United States was at Abraham Lincoln's funeral.

The most famous caparisoned horse at Arlington was a spirited black Morgan-American Quarter horse, named Black Jack after the famous World War I Commander of U.S. forces John "Black Jack" Pershing. Brought east in 1953 from a base in Nevada, Black Jack was stabled at Fort Myer, which borders the western edge of Arlington, and served for twenty years. In that time he walked behind more than one thousand caissons—most famously at the burial of the assassinated president John Fitzgerald Kennedy, where his high energy was seen by many as representative of the youthfulness of the slain president.

President Kennedy had visited Arlington in the spring of 1963. A young guide stood with him on the hillside just below Arlington House. Looking east across the Potomac River pointing out Memorial Bridge, he told the president about the significance of the bridge's placement, linking the Lincoln Memorial to Arlington House and intended as a symbolic "mend" between Robert E. Lee and Abraham Lincoln. With Washington's trees in full blossom, Kennedy remarked: "I could stay up here forever."

Seven months later, President Kennedy was cut down by an assassin's bullets. Where he'd stood that previous spring, his remains now rest. A small gas-fired "eternal flame" burns in the center of a rough-cut stone memorial. His funeral, televised to millions around the world, swelled the number of tourists visiting Arlington from one million a year to more than nine million in the first six months following his burial. Each year the numbers continue to increase.

In addition to President Kennedy, Arlington is the burial place of one other president, William Taft. To be buried at Arlington, a person must have served the country as a member of the armed forces, an elected official, or in a high-level government position such as a Supreme Court justice.

Monuments throughout Arlington's grounds commemorate the nation's military history and other events, from the memorial to Unknown Civil War Dead and the Confederate Memorial to monuments marking the Space Shuttle Challenger accident and the September 11, 2001 attack on the Pentagon.

Anita Newcomb McGee, the only woman with the rank of assistant surgeon of the U.S. Army, was responsible for the creation of a monument to nurses who served in the Spanish-American War and World War I. The ten-foot-tall granite sculpture was dedicated in 1938. Originally only those nurses in the army and navy were recognized, but in 1971 a rededication was made to include all military nurses.

Maintenance of Arlington's grounds is never ending. Headstones are cleaned, lawns mowed, trees are pruned or removed. Holes for burials are dug precisely and awnings and chairs for family and guests set up—all to exacting standards and carefully choreographed to flow with the twenty or so ceremonies that take place every day.

Each year on the day before Memorial Day, young soldiers, marines, airmen, navy, and coast guard place small American flags in the ground in front of each headstone. This tradition, known as "flags" or "flags in" started in 1948 when the Old Guard took over the guarding of the Tomb of the Unknowns. More than three thousand servicemen and servicewomen participate, placing more than a quarter of a million flags in one day. The flags are placed at uniform height and one boot length from the headstone. As in so many things at Arlington National Cemetery, precision and routine pay respect to those who served this country.

Precision governs the ritual followed by the guard at the Tomb of the Unknowns, one of the most compelling sights at Arlington. In keeping with the highest military honor, the twenty-one-gun salute, the guard walks twenty-one steps on the mat in front of the Tomb, followed by a twenty-one-second pause, before returning twenty-one paces back. On each pass the guard shoulders the rifle on the outside toward the public in symbolic protection of the unknowns. During the hot summer months, the guard is changed every thirty minutes. It is an hour in winter. When a change of guard is posted, a rigorous, tightly choreographed rifle inspection takes place.

Over the years the guards' uniform has changed from a simple khaki shirt, tie, and trousers to the current more formal wool jacket and pants. The soles of the guards' shoes are built up to make the legs appear straighter, the bright yellow outside stripe on the pants enhancing the effect. The inside heels protrude to make for a more resounding clap when brought together. During the warmer months the guards wear white cotton gloves, sprayed with water to prevent loss of grip. Placement of belt loops and belt, folds in the jacket, and the shine on the shoes (also known as the "Kiwi") are done to strict guidelines to maintain an exact uniform look between all tomb guards.

More than six thousand burials take place each year at Arlington. Some are for retired servicemen and servicewomen. Others are for those killed in action in the nation's current conflicts in Iraq and Afghanistan. A separate section of the cemetery, Section 60, is set aside for them.

For all, burial at Arlington National Cemetery is among the highest honor accorded those who served their country. All burials are given full honors, including the bugler sounding taps, a seven-member firing squad firing three volleys, and a band playing a final salute. And every burial ends with the simplest and most moving of ceremonies: the flag draped on the coffin being carefully removed, folded into a tricorn, and presented to the family.

Each day at Arlington fills the senses. From the distant noise of mowers and trimmers to the soft clip-clop of horses pulling caissons; from the smell of blossoms in spring to fallen leaves in the fall; from the sharp report of rifle and cannon volleys to the heart-stopping sound of taps—all are a part of paying honor to those who lie in the nation's most hallowed grounds.

TIMELINE

George Washington Parke Custis,
photographed in 1844

1781 ∽ George Washington Parke Custis born (April 30).

1802 ∽ Parke Custis begins construction of Arlington House on land overlooking the Potomac River and Washington, D.C., inherited from his father.

1831 ∽ Parke Custis's daughter, Mary Anna Randolph Custis, marries Robert E. Lee at Arlington (June 30).

1857 ∽ George Washington Parke Custis dies, leaving Arlington House and its estates to daughter Mary Lee.

1861–65 American Civil War

1861 ∽ Robert E. Lee resigns from the U.S. Army and joins the Confederacy (April 20). Union soldiers occupy Arlington.

1864 ∽ U.S. government confiscates Arlington House and its property when Mary Lee fails to appear in person to pay taxes. The government purchases Arlington at auction for $26,802 (January) and designates the property a cemetery. Private William H. Christman is the first soldier buried at Arlington (May 13). More than one thousand freed slaves are given land in a portion of the property that would become known as Freedman's Village.

1882 ∽ U.S. Supreme Court rules that Arlington had been seized illegally and orders the property returned to the Lee family. In March 1883 Robert and Mary Lee's son, George Washington Custis Lee, agrees to sell the property to the U.S. government for $150,000.

1892 ∽ The first Revolutionary War dead are reburied at Arlington.

1898 ∽ Spanish-American War

1914–18 World War I. The United States enters the war in 1917.

1920 ∽ Arlington Memorial Amphitheater opens, replacing a smaller public space behind Arlington House.

1921 ∽ The Tomb of the Unknowns is established when an unidentified U.S. soldier from World War I is buried at a ceremony presided over by President Warren G. Harding (November 11, Veterans Day).

1925 ∽ Arlington House becomes a memorial to George Washington Parke Custis and Robert E. Lee.

1930 ∽ William H. Taft is the first U.S president buried at Arlington (March).

1937 ∽ Twenty-four-hour guard begins at the Tomb of the Unknowns.

1939–45 World War II. The United States enters the war in 1941.

1950–53 Korean War

1958 ∽ Unidentified soldiers from World War II and the Korean War are buried alongside the World War I unknown at the Tomb of the Unknowns (May 30, Memorial Day).

1959–75 Vietnam War. United States combat troops serve in Vietnam beginning in 1965.

1963 ∽ President John F. Kennedy is assassinated and buried at Arlington (November 25).

1984 ∽ Unknown soldier from Vietnam is buried at the Tomb of the Unknowns (May 28, Memorial Day). The Vietnam unknown is later identified as 1st Lieutenant Michael Joseph Blassie and reburied in his home state of Missouri.

1990–91 Persian Gulf War

1996 ∽ Sergeant Heather Lynn Johnsen becomes the first female tomb guard to serve at Arlington.

2001 ∽ Afghan War begins.

2003 ∽ Iraq War begins. Section 60, a five-acre parcel, is opened for Iraq and Afghan war veterans.

More than 300,000 people are buried at Arlington National Cemetery. Among them are the following:

Medgar Evers, World War II veteran and Civil Rights activist

Samuel Dashiell Hammett, World War I and II veteran and novelist

Oliver Wendell Holmes, Civil War veteran and Supreme Court Justice

Daniel "Chappie" James Jr., first African-American four-star general, U.S.A.F.

John F. Kennedy, 35th President of the United States

Robert F. Kennedy, Attorney General, and **Edward M. Kennedy**, Senator —brothers of President John F. Kennedy

Joe Louis, U.S. Army veteran and boxer

Anita Newcomb McGee, founder of Army Nurses Corps

Audie Murphy, most decorated World War II veteran

Admiral Robert E. Peary, Medal of Honor recipient and polar explorer

John Wesley Powell, Civil War veteran and first explorer of the Grand Canyon

William H. Taft, 27th President of the United States

There are numerous memorials at Arlington commemorating events in the nation's military and political history, including:

Unknown Civil War Dead

Confederate Monument

Rough Riders Memorial

U.S.S. *Maine* Memorial

U.S. Coast Guard Memorial

Women in Military Service for America Memorial

Battle of the Bulge Memorial

Space Shuttle Challenger Memorial

Pan Am Flight 103 Memorial

Pentagon 9/11 Memorial

Freedman's Villiage, Arlington, Va.

In its early history as home to George Washington Parke Custis, Arlington was a 1,100-acre plantation whose field work was done by slaves. In his will, Parke Custis decreed that five years after his death (which took place in 1857), all slaves at Arlington would be given $50 and set free. However at that time the Union Army and U.S. government had seized the property, which nullified the will.

Freedman's Village (above), a collection of two-family, wood-framed homes, was built during the Civil War for the slaves working at Arlington and some of the freed slaves from southern states. Some worked for the Union Army, including digging graves for the fallen soldiers. Grave markers with "U.S.C.T" (U.S. Colored Troops) designated those who fought and died while serving in the Union Army. Three were Medal of Honor recipients. Slaves who died while at Freedman's Village were buried with a simple headstone reading either "Citizen" or "Civilian." Freedman's Village existed for thirty years.

AUTHOR'S NOTE

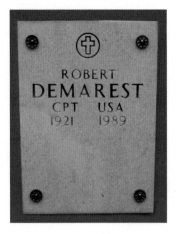

Arlington National Cemetery grew in importance to me the day my father was laid to rest there. Watching the burial with full military honors is a moment seared into my memory. Each time I visit the grounds and hear the crack of the rifles and taps sounded, I'm taken back to that spring day in 1989. A few years later, when I became an official artist for the U.S. Coast Guard, documenting many aspects of their work, including covering a U.S.C.G. funeral at Arlington, I realized I had to do a book on this special place.

Arlington is about more than those buried there. Throughout the grounds, one sees young saplings taking root near ancient oaks and maples towering above the undulating landscape of hedges and monuments. Every year nature has its own story of life and death to tell, from the beauty of spring buds and flowers to the brilliant fall leaves and eventual snow-covered grounds. In telling this story, I chose to use a red oak as a sort-of timeline for the more than two-hundred-year history of Arlington. The opening illustration shows George Washington Parke Custis standing next to a young oak as it establishes its own footing. The vantage point changes as the tree grows, giving the reader a different perspective over time. Because there is no one central tree with a view of all of the grounds, animals become the vehicle to continue the tour. In the last painting, as the tree nears its own end, we see new saplings establishing their roots to symbolize the continued oversight of these hallowed grounds.

It is not only the major sights and monuments that tell Arlington's story. Every marker is a story unto itself, and to truly appreciate Arlington is to explore the far corners of the cemetery. For me, spending time with the Honor Guard both at the Tomb of the Unknowns and at Ft. Myer where the caissons and horses are kept was a privilege I will always cherish. I find with each return visit the desire to keep wandering, taking time to read the random headstones as a way to touch Arlington more intimately.

ACKNOWLEDGMENTS

This book would not be possible were it not for the generous help of the following people:

Administration, Arlington National Cemetery: Vicki Tanner, Phyllis White.

Bill Halainen, writer/editor, National Park Service

National Park Service/Arlington House: Kendall Thompson.

Old Guard, 3rd Army Infantry, Ft. Myer, VA: Major Joel Lindeman, Sergeant Brian Parker, Sergeant Nancy Van Der Weide.

U.S. Army Public Affairs: Harrison Sarles, Jennifer K. Yancey.

RECOMMENDED READING

Arlington National Cemetery Commemorative Project, *Where Valor Rests: Arlington National Cemetery*. Washington, D.C., 2007: National Geographic Society.

Dieterle, Lorraine (photographer), *Arlington National Cemetery: A Nation's Story Carved in Stone*. Petaluma, CA, 2001: Pomegranate Communications, Inc.

Arlington House: A Guide to Arlington House, The Robert E. Lee Memorial, Virginia. Washington, D.C., 1985: National Park Service/U.S. Department of the Interior.

Dodge, George, *Arlington National Cemetery: Images of America*. San Francisco CA/Charleston SC, 2006: Arcadia Publishing.

WEBSITES

Arlington National Cemetery: www.arlingtonnationalcemetery.org
National Park Service: www.nps.gov
Chris Demarest: www.pbase.com/chrisdemarest